First Look: Science

From Little Acorns ...
A First Look at the Life Cycle of a Tree

by Sam Godwin   illustrated by Simone Abel

Thanks to our reading adviser:

Susan Kesselring, M.A., Literacy Educator
Rosemount-Apple Valley-Eagan (Minnesota) School District

PICTURE WINDOW BOOKS
Minneapolis, Minnesota

First American edition published in 2005 by
Picture Window Books
5115 Excelsior Boulevard
Suite 232
Minneapolis, MN 55416
877-845-8392
www.picturewindowbooks.com

First Published in Great Britain in 2001 by Hodder Wayland,
Hodder Children's Books
A division of Hodder Headline Limited
338 Euston Road
London NW1 3BH

Printed in the United States of America.

Library of Congress Cataloging-in-Publication Data
Godwin, Sam.
From little acorns … : a first look at the life cycle of a tree / by
Sam Godwin ; illustrated by Simone Abel.
p. cm. — (First look : science)
ISBN 1-4048-0658-X (hardcover)
1. Oak—Life cycles—Juvenile literature. I. Abel, Simone, ill.
II. Title. III. Series.
QK495.F14G64 2005
571.8'2346—dc22   2004007311

For Fleur Pirotta – SG

For Aunty Ruth and Uncle Peter – SA

It is autumn. In the woods, acorns

Mommy, something hit me on the head!

BOING!

4

Hidden safely under a blanket of leaves,

What's an acorn, Mommy?

7

Autumn turns to winter. The acorn lies asleep.

8

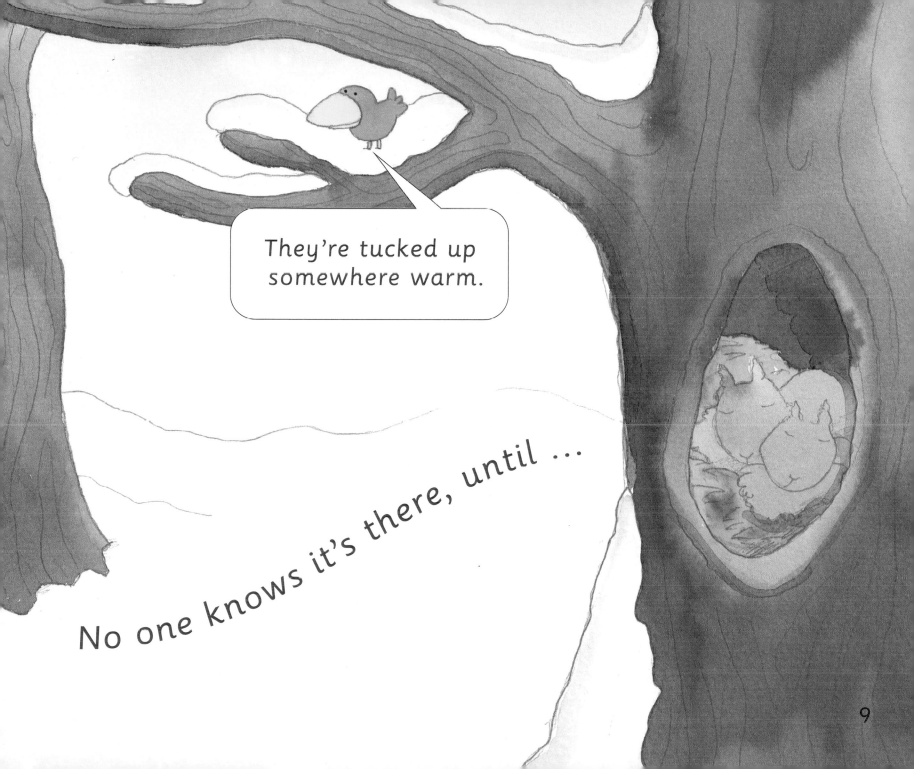

spring arrives. The air is warm and damp.

Mommy, has the little acorn grown leaves?

A seedling grows from the acorn.

Yes. Let's hope the caterpillars don't nibble at them.

After about three years, the seedling will

grow into a sapling.

Over 30 years, the branches will get thicker.

This oak tree is tall!

14

The sapling will become an oak tree.

Wow! It started as a little acorn.

17

the small brown flowers become acorns.

19

Then the acorns fall to the ground.

21

Most of the acorns are eaten by animals.

But a few survive and grow roots.

With a little luck, each acorn will grow up

24

Yes, we do. We share it with lots of other creatures.

during its lifetime.

27

The Oak Tree Life Cycle

1 In late autumn, an acorn falls from an adult oak tree. The leaves fall, too.

8 In early autumn, there are acorns on the tree.

7 In late spring, the tree grows flowers.

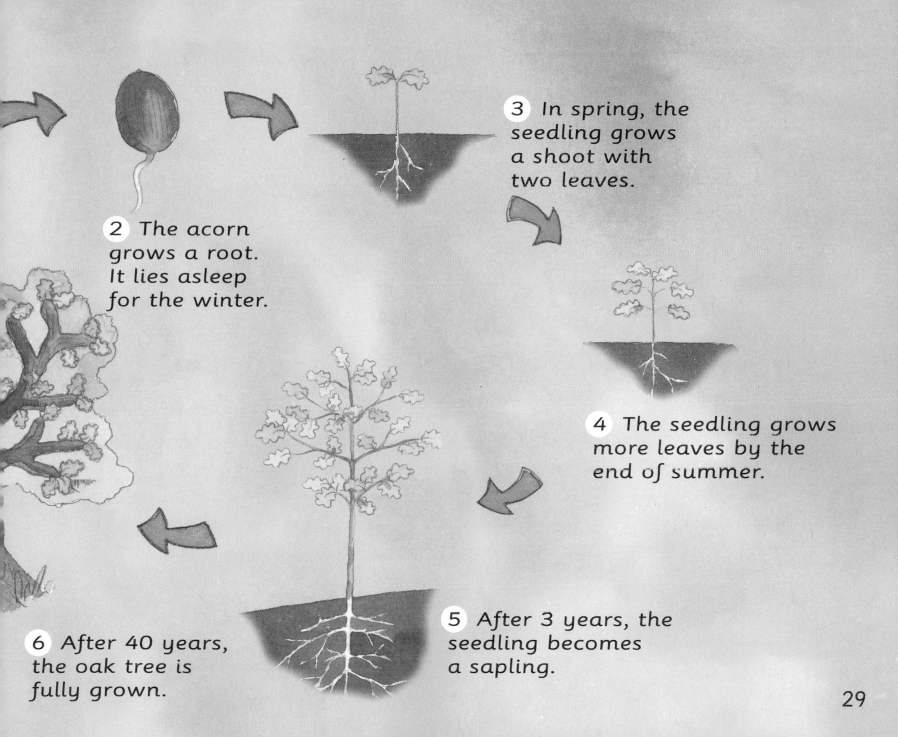

2 The acorn grows a root. It lies asleep for the winter.

3 In spring, the seedling grows a shoot with two leaves.

4 The seedling grows more leaves by the end of summer.

5 After 3 years, the seedling becomes a sapling.

6 After 40 years, the oak tree is fully grown.

29

Useful Words

Acorn

The fruit of an oak tree.

Bark

The rough brown part of a tree trunk.

Catkins

Male flowers, full of pollen.

Roots

The parts of a plant that hold it in the soil.

Sapling

A young tree. It is too young to make seeds of its own.

Seed

Part of a flower that will grow into a new plant.

Seedling

A small plant with a green, leafy shoot.

Fun Facts

 In the fall, a mature oak tree will lose about 700,000 leaves.

 There are between 500 and 600 types of oak trees in the world.

 Oak trees are struck by lightning more than any other kind of tree.

 Oak trees can live more than 200 years.

To Learn More

At the Library

Danzig, Marsha T. *The Tiniest Acorn: A Story to Grow by*. Hollywood, Fla.: Frederick Fell, 1999.

Greeley, Valerie. *The Acorn's Story*. New York: Macmillan Pub. Co., 1994.

Owen, Oliver S. *Acorn to Oak Tree*. Edina, Minn.: Abdo & Daughters, 1994.

On the Web

FactHound offers a safe, fun way to find Web sites related to this book. All of the sites on FactHound have been researched by our staff. *www.facthound.com*

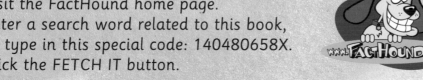

1. Visit the FactHound home page.
2. Enter a search word related to this book, or type in this special code: 140480658X.
3. Click the FETCH IT button.

Your trusty FactHound will fetch the best Web sites for you!

Index

Look for all the books in this series:

A Seed in Need
A First Look at the Plant Cycle

And Everyone Shouted, "Pull!"
A First Look at Forces of Motion

From Little Acorns ...
A First Look at the Life Cycle of a Tree

Paint a Sun in the Sky
A First Look at the Seasons

Take a Walk on a Rainbow
A First Look at Color

The Case of the Missing Caterpillar
A First Look at the Life Cycle of a Butterfly

The Drop Goes Plop
A First Look at the Water Cycle

The Hen Can't Help It
A First Look at the Life Cycle of a Chicken

The Trouble with Tadpoles
A First Look at the Life Cycle of a Frog